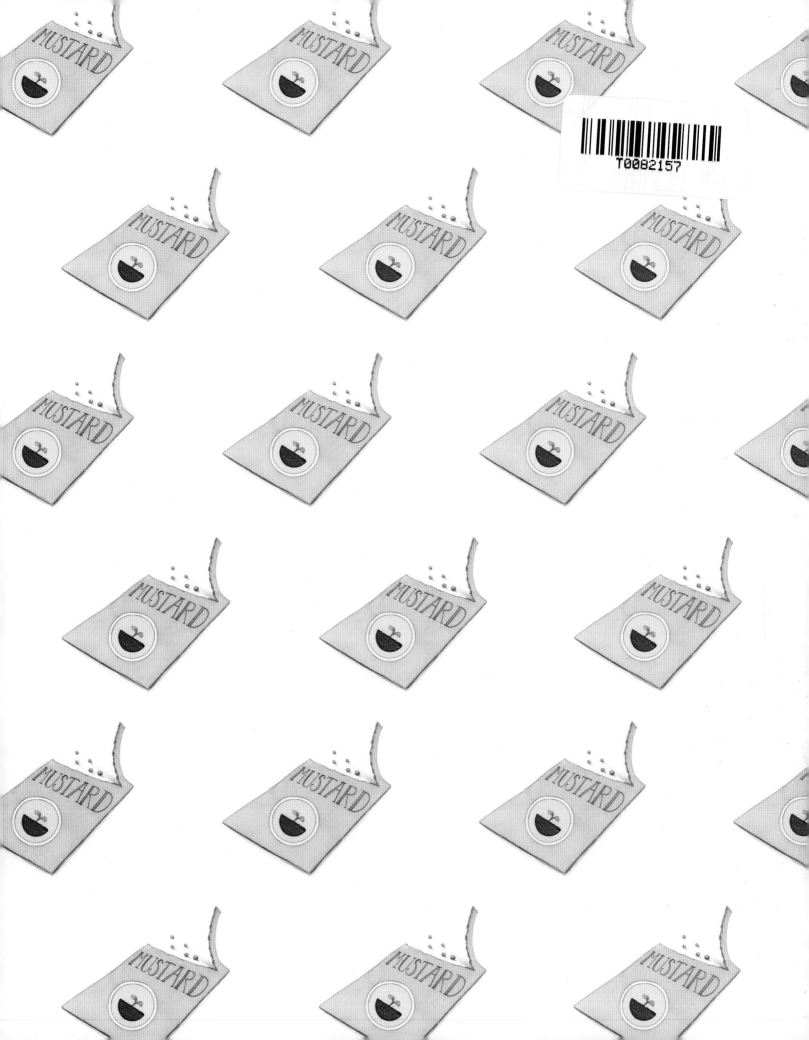

The Marvelous
Mustard Seed

The Marvelous
Mustard Seed

Amy-Jill Levine &
Sandy Eisenberg Sasso

Illustrated by Margaux Meganck

flyaway
books
Louisville, Kentucky

© 2018 Amy-Jill Levine and Sandy Eisenberg Sasso
Illustrations © 2018 Margaux Meganck

First edition
Published by Flyaway Books
Louisville, Kentucky

   19 20 21 22 23 24 25 26 27—10 9 8 7 6 5 4 3 2

Book design by Allison Taylor
Cover design by Allison Taylor
Cover illustration by Margaux Meganck

Library of Congress Cataloging-in-Publication Data
Names: Levine, Amy-Jill, 1956- author. | Meganck, Margaux, illustrator.
Title: The marvelous mustard seed / Amy-Jill Levine and Sandy Eisenberg Sasso
   ; illustrations by Margaux Meganck.
Description: First edition. | Louisville, Kentucky : Flyaway Books, [2018] |
   Audience: Age 4-8. | Audience: K to Grade 3.
Identifiers: LCCN 2017049203 | ISBN 9780664262754 (hbk. : alk. paper)
Subjects: LCSH: Mustard seed (Parable)--Juvenile literature. |
   Mustard--Seeds--Life cycles--Juvenile literature.
Classification: LCC BT378.M8 L48 2018 | DDC 226.8/06--dc23 LC record
   available at https://lccn.loc.gov/2017049203

PRINTED IN CHINA

Most Flyaway Books are available at special quantity discounts when
purchased in bulk by corporations, organizations, and special-interest groups.
For more information, please e-mail SpecialSales@flyawaybooks.com.

A child plants a mustard seed in an empty garden.
It is an itty-bitty seed.
It isn't anything very special—yet.

Mustard seeds are so small
that you have to look hard to see them.

You have to look so hard to see them
that you need to get really close.

There is not much to be done with a single teeny-weeny seed.

You can't eat it

or wear it.

You can't
take it for
a walk

or cuddle with it.

You can't write or blow bubbles with it.

The only thing you can do is plant it in the soil.

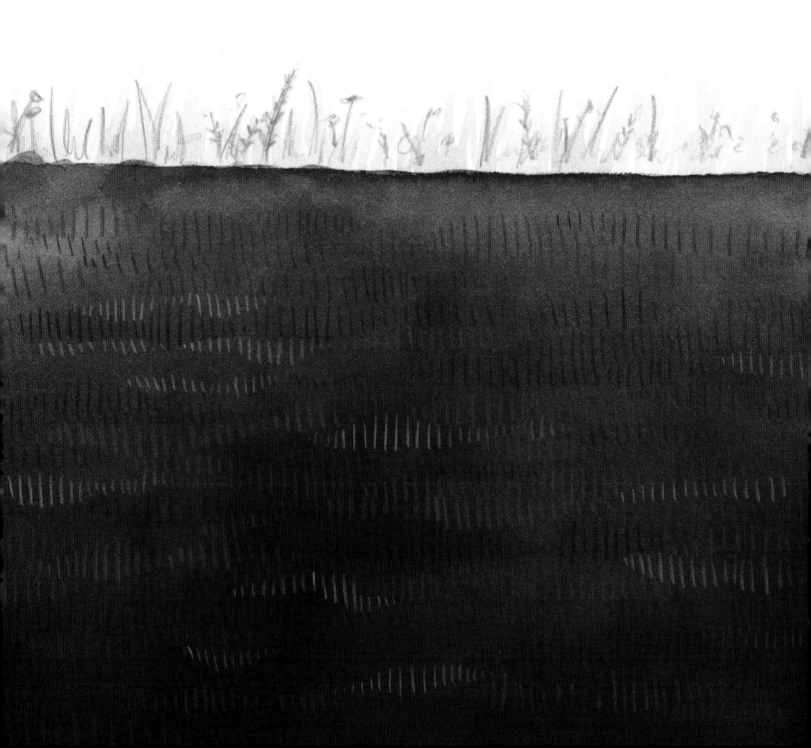

Then the rain falls and the sun shines,

and things begin to happen in the earth

But no matter how hard you look

or how close you get,

MUSTARD

you can't see
the tiny seed.

The seed is hidden,

down with the moles,

down,
down with the ants,

down,

down,

down with
the earthworms.

Then it happens!

In the place of the
little bitty seed,

up comes a shoot,

up,

up comes
a sprout.

Up, **up, up** comes a bush,

…but it doesn't stop there.

It grows, and it grows, and it grows…

until it becomes a
humongous tree.

Birds make their
nests there.

The neighbors exclaim,

A mustard tree?

Amazing!

Birds resting there?

Acorns grow into big oak trees.

Cedars have
trunks that you
can't fit your
arms around.

Mustard plants
are just ordinary
bushes.

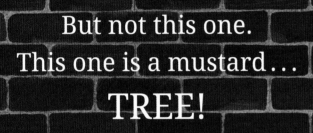

But not this one.
This one is a mustard...
TREE!

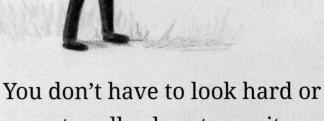

You don't have to look hard or
get really close to see it.

It is right in front of you.

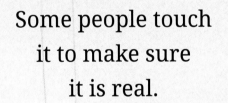

Some people touch
it to make sure
it is real.

Others sit under
its branches.

They take the pods from
the tree and remove the
seeds and make spices.

They take the mustard
leaves and the seeds
and make medicine.

The spices and the medicine are there for everyone.

The kingdom of God
is like a mustard seed in the garden,
right outside our windows,

growing from

ittsy-bittsy, teensy-weensy

to

colossal,

from

impossible to see

to

unable to miss.

The tree is
so gigantic;
it's a wonder!

It is not at all what we expect to find.

And yet there it is,
surprising us,
helping us to imagine what can be…

but isn't . . .

yet!

A Note to Parents and Teachers

The word "parable" comes from two Greek words: *para*—as in parallel—means to put something side by side; *balo* means to cast or to throw. Thus a parable casts two images side by side. When we look at the connection between what happens in the story and what happens in our own lives, we begin to see new things. But parables are more than simple comparisons. A parable asks us to think about very important matters: our relationships with others, our place in the world, how we can be better people. A parable can challenge us to see that there is more to life than we had imagined.

The parable of the Mustard Seed appears three times in the New Testament, in the Gospels of Matthew (13:31–32), Mark (4:30–32), and Luke (13:18–19). Each version is slightly different, but this should not be surprising. Storytellers often tell the same story with different words.

The same story can also provoke different responses. Children will see things that adults do not, and vice versa. In Christianity, this parable receives multiple interpretations. Some readers see a contrast between the small seed and the very large tree and therefore find a message of the miraculous growth of the church or of personal faith. Others find a message of encouragement: from tiny seeds do giant trees bloom. Jesus also speaks of faith "the size of a mustard seed" that can move mountains (Matt. 17:20; see also Luke 17:6). Because mustard seeds do not grow into giant trees but rather into small bushes, some interpreters find a message about resurrection or eternal life when human bodies become perfect and glorious. Some readers conclude that the birds represent the gentile nations who flock to the limbs of the church. Still others, more practically, note that mustard has substantial medicinal and culinary properties and so recognize that even a weed can be beneficial. All these readings, and the many others developed over the past two thousand years, have merit.

Sometimes, however, interpreters see what is not there. Some Christian interpreters have suggested that mustard seeds are "unclean" and that the parable therefore does away with Jewish dietary laws (sometimes called "keeping kosher"). This is an incorrect reading: Jews appreciate mustard on a hot dog (preferably Hebrew National) just as much as anyone else.

Our presentation of these parables does not intend to erase the good readings that have been offered; nor do we offer a singular "right" reading. Rather, we seek to add a new understanding based on what we imagine Jesus' original audiences might have heard. That audience, of Jewish people listening to a Jewish storyteller, would have expected a parable to challenge them. There is no challenge in hearing that from small beginnings come great things. They would not likely have thought that the seed represented faith, the gospel, or the Christ. It would not have occurred to them that the tree is the church, or the birds, or the gentiles. Parables were not originally allegories, with every element in the story containing secret meaning. Parables can open up our imagination, if we let them.

Consider reading the story with these questions in mind:

Where are you in this story? Are you like the children who have a mustard seed? What should you do with this seed? If you put it in the ground, what might happen to it? How long will it take to sprout? Will it grow into a weed, or a flower, or a beanstalk, or a giant tree? Will your seed become a home for others, a sanctuary for birds, a place where people can find medicine or spices? What can one tiny seed do? And what happens if no one plants it?

Or perhaps you are the seed. I wonder if you ever feel like the mustard seed in the story? No one expects very much of you, because you are so little. No one thinks you can do anything very big and important, because you are so young. You may not be a giant tree now, but just wait; because once you get started, there is no stopping you.

Or perhaps, just perhaps, something wonderful and beautiful and surprising is in your own backyard, or in the widow box, or in a paper cup filled with dirt in which you planted one tiny seed. Everything is in place, if our imagination allows.

Amy-Jill Levine

is University Professor of New Testament and Jewish Studies, Mary Jane Werthan Professor of Jewish Studies, and Professor of New Testament Studies at Vanderbilt University. For more details on the parables, see her book *Short Stories by Jesus: The Enigmatic Parables of a Controversial Rabbi* (New York: HarperOne, 2014).

Sandy Eisenberg Sasso

is Rabbi Emerita of Congregation Beth-El Zedeck and an author of many award-winning children's books, including *Who Counts? 100 Sheep, 10 Coins, and 2 Sons* (with Amy-Jill Levine). She is also the author of *Midrash—Reading the Bible with Question Marks* (Brewster, MA: Paraclete Press, 2013).

Margaux Meganck

is a freelance artist and children's book illustrator in Portland, Oregon. She is a member of the Society of Children's Book Writers and Illustrators. To see more of her work, visit www.margauxmeganck.com.

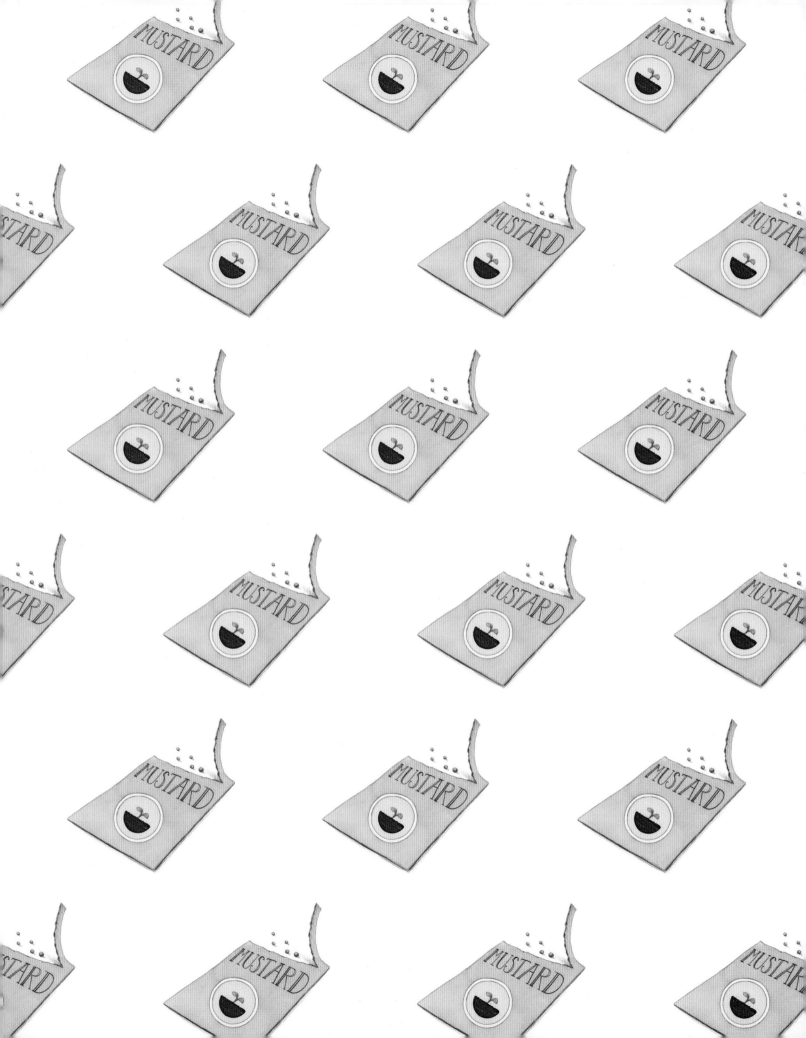